Unsalted Blue Sunrise

Poems of Lake Michigan

Kathryn P. Haydon

Prairie Cloud Press

Cover Design By: Lily and Russell Jenkins
Book Design By: Julie Hodgins

ISBN: 978-0-9963856-1-9

Prairie Cloud Press
Chicago

Proudly printed in the United States of America.

To JH
Thank you for believing in me always,
and for bringing me back to the lake.

Poems

From a fixed spot on the bluff, I watch Lake Michigan. On some days I sweat and on others, my fingers freeze around the pencil. It has to be a pencil.

For a year, I walk to the lake each day to write a poem—inspired by a small, handmade book. My aunt's friend positioned a camera in her Lake Shore Drive apartment window to capture Lake Michigan's almost unbelievable daily shape-shifts. She curated a selection of these photos into a book that prompted me to embark on a similar project, but with poetry.

Claude Monet painted the same wheatstacks over the arc of a year, capturing texture, color, and mood. He made thirty paintings. The book you are holding is a collection of forty-five poems, written over four seasons at the lakeshore.

Why do we revisit a singular subject—the lake or a field of wheat? What do we learn about ourselves, our lives? Do we change our minds?

Perhaps this book will provide answers or, better yet, spark more questions and your own study of a ravine, a pine, or a patch of sky outside your window.

For me a landscape hardly exists at all as a landscape,
because its appearance is constantly changing;
but it lives by virtue of its surroundings,
the air and the light which vary continually.

—Claude Monet

My paintings repeat a feeling about Lake Michigan,
or water, or fields . . . It's more like a poem . . .
and that's what I want to paint.

—Joan Mitchell, *Joan Mitchell:*
   Portrait of an Abstract Painter

The plumes of steamboat smoke and the white canvas of sailboats met the eye as twilight glimmered and failed, and a red rim of a big slow moon pushed up the horizon where the sky line touched the water line of Lake Michigan. The stars came out and a silver sheen glistened on the lake waves breaking and rippling on the beach sand.

—Carl Sandburg, *Abraham Lincoln: The Prairie Years* II

Unsalted Blue Sunrise

Benches stretch across shoreline park,
           set apart
                      for solitude.

I count twelve, twenty-two
           they all
                      face east.

We who sit, a soundless congregation
           the lake,
                      a sermon in waves.

In two dimensions,
lake and sky meet in their se-
cret horizon land.

We believe the fish
stories our eyes sing at bed-
time, lulled in lace.

Coffee gathers words
that eavesdrop on the real world
unspool its soft lies.

Unsalted Blue Sunrise

The gentle coming and going waves
croon in my ears this morning

Crescendo and diminuendo like billowy smoke
yawn in these early hours

Coral morning light lingers above the horizon
thoughts stretch across time

I'm loath to return to ones and zeroes
to zeroes and never the one.

She wears her veil—
humidity
drapes horizon,
fills space.

She plays coy,
as if we can't see her
blush blue
in hazy sunshine.

Unsalted Blue Sunrise

The flock
of black birds
steers
against wind,
unswerving.
Lake trembles
in clock's
wake.

I used to stand
each evening on the back porch
waiting for the pink moment—
alpenglow.

Now the lake spreads
its rose-colored fondant
neatly from shore
to level horizon.

Talkers complain
when it's gray;
birds perch at attention,
salute sun's blushing descent.

Unsalted Blue Sunrise

To take the wrong turn
arrive at the pool
of minnows
where ancient seagrass
boils in afternoon sun.

When my voice shudders
smoke rises on blue wind
summons poets and painters
from far-off bluffs
to stand at attention and weep.

After Federico García Lorca,
"Pequeño poema infinito"

You imagine storms—
    wood boat
        churning
    directionless.

But anchor
    dropped
        in dangerous
    waters.

Unmoored, freedom.

Unsalted Blue Sunrise

Moon-
     drops
     bathe
        tonight.
Moon
     drips
     its ribbons
        onto
slow-
dancing

waves
     whispering
     secrets. Locust buzz
deafening.

August. Muggy bridge
to a cold-numbed nose.

Wind whips up whitecaps,
azure mirage.

Jagged waves refract thoughts
and a gray owl sings hollow.

At least we don't spit saltwater
swimming in the lake.

Unsalted Blue Sunrise

A gull feather lands
            at the foot of the birch.

Two squirrels race
            up parchment skin.

A thousand birds sing coded songs
            from a single branch—

the birch tells no one
            their secrets.

My fingers trace
            the braille of the bark.

A man taps his tambourine
            to metronome waves.

Questions roast
            in the afternoon sunshine

and answers
are jammed
in a glass mason jar.

Hazy moon shines
a single headlight in fog

drips streams of honey
onto slow-dancing waves

Locusts whisper final
strains of summer

ravaging the crops
we saved for canning

They flipped summer's off switch
as we passed through the equinox
right on cue

On cue
the wind called up waves
and the lake churned

Heavy not menacing clouds
saunter above swells
Goodyear blimp circles the stadium

That narrow portal
of peach light on the horizon
swiftly shrinks to midnight.

One paper-white sailboat
traces horizon's straight edge
blends with skyline
pokes in and out of cotton clouds.

Beach season has passed
but water never closes
for bold mariners
and those who cling to summer.

Sailboat hangs warm
while Speedos
and woolen hats
wade into winter.

Unsalted Blue Sunrise

The lake prepares for winter
paws at the smoke-gray sky
licks cream-frothed
clouds like open wounds.
The waves drip out "Taps"
day is done, sun is gone.

       I zip up my thoughts.

Its breath steams.
The lake's breath
steams. The lake's
breath is steaming.

Near the center
of the ice-edged shore
a little bird swims.
He swims near
the ragged
rocky ice-edge.

Heavy clouds press the horizon.
Heavy clouds
press down. But the lake's breath
steams and a little bird swims.

After William Carlos Williams

Unsalted Blue Sunrise

If I hadn't
had to remove my mittens
to write this poem

If pre-winter air wasn't
nipping at my fingertips

If maples and elms weren't
golden and burnt orange

I might wish I'm standing
on an island casting
muffled dreams at the Pacific.

The gull pushes
currents of wind
one linebacker
against the world.

Beach bathers long gone
weekend sailors don't
brave whitecaps
and gathering storms.

Wind spits freshwater spray
and I brace
my gaze on a single
sliver of light.

Unsalted Blue Sunrise

I wish to speak to the manager.
These waters do not meet
seasonal expectations.
I demand a refund on today's view.
Store credit will not suffice.

The lake deceives with color,
her lying tongue lashing cold.
A mislabeled shelf—
false advertising!
It tempted me with summer.

The mourning dove calls
    and sparrows croon

If I closed my eyes and you
    played me the soundtrack
        I'd guess summer

Spring should floor it to pass on the left
    the polar swimmers
        in knit hats and bikinis
    splashing in the lake
        with migratory birds

We're stuck behind
    the lowered gates
        and the freight train
           rumbles on

Unsalted Blue Sunrise

Today an iridescent afternoon.

Pearly rose and blue silk
stretch across the mirror.

For several yesterdays, frigid—
negative zero I think.

But now ice wedges shrink,
vanished remnants of arctic chill.

A white gull flees the horizon
of winter's dark abyss.

We won't look
    at the water
    in the space
    below the sun

In that single spot
    the lake is brilliant
    and blinding

We switch our gaze
onto dark waves.

White seagull flies
through

stinging winter air
she

glides in freedom
no

fear of cold
or

losing her way
under

plum canopy sky

What guides
her

dive for food?
Faith

in lake's provision
an

etched V
against

darkening sky.

The tempest
    spits
trees pound
    their fists
        onto haphazard
clouds

Our loveless
    lives
        blacken
    the earth

Answer
    the surging lake
with the roaring
    race of the sky

The law of love
    rolling the clouds
sewn into the hem of life

Let it come down.

Unsalted Blue Sunrise

Lake and sky sewn together in a somber cloud. Color of cement where people fell as he trained his scope on the procession, heart locked in shadow. Cardinal stares at me sternly. I hear laughter rise above bluffs as children splash on shore. The red bird turns and dares me to understand his message. Day lily seeds.

The ghost
lurking
in misty sky
curtain
of monotonous
gray
Sky water
blends
with lake water
clouds
spray teardrops
fuse
into ice

Trudging
through sand
to mourn
fifty-seven alewives
washed up on shore.
Tears fall

on the altar
of silver bodies
in noontime sun.

The cantor says
the Talmud says
a funeral procession
must yield
to a wedding march.
You wade

ten inches east
water pools
around your feet
and little fish nibble
your ankles.

From   floor   of   lake
to ceiling of sky
every glance
a different shade—
robin's egg   cornflower   murky deep Aegean.

Blues   boil   and   froth
in human hearts:
arsenic   bile   fear
splash
  burning
    sadness.

A   kiss   of   honeydew
                    skyline   sings   of   light.

Unsalted Blue Sunrise

From the bluff, the lake
sprawls elegant
in her patina of sunshine

as murky sand-churned
waters explode on rocks,
gun toward the beach.

My aunt said
        the compass is broken
needle pointing south
we will never walk
the flowing lines again

The moon disagrees
        and floods crushed
petals with a soft halo
the color of a kiss

Birds beat their wings
        in leftover winter wind
glide toward pink
magnolia blossoms

Unsalted Blue Sunrise

The clouds
dressed her today
in the blue ombré gown
striped with emerald and sunshine.
Her skirts twirl in the breeze
carefree in ballet slippers
spinning in the yard.

Lake dimples
where she smiles

Over there where
the waterbirds flock

Beguiling, the lake
her dimple and her wink

Unsalted Blue Sunrise

Turns out that clouds
are snowbirds too
retired Midwesterners

who migrate and gather
in the warmest spot.

Today a cottony cluster
huddles over falling
mercury pooling far
from snow-covered land

where frozen fingers gnarl
around a pencil stub.

I expect an agitated
            lake,
to-do list
            pressing

on the water
            as it presses
on my thoughts.

Royal blue waves
            convey
lily-white sailboats,
            serene.

Unsalted Blue Sunrise

We leap from the sandbar
and swim farther into the lake
where a thousand smelt
encircle our toes
and water turns to golden honey
spinning plaster on dull legs

We cup our hands to scoop
sweet mouthfuls
inch forward then back
Our sticky lips seal
legs in casts—floating
upturned like petrified bees

I had a necklace
made of lapis lazuli
from Chile.

The skyline strip of her
looks like lapis—
blue set in aqua.

My mom wears
the necklace now
but she will always

shimmer
as she dangles
from the shore.

Unsalted Blue Sunrise

If I could walk on the water
I'd stride onto crashing waves

After a mile or so I'd step into sky
where two grays become one

and disappear behind the cloud curtain
to watch water birds at sunset

The dinner bell echoes faintly
but I'm trapped in this dream

Shattered glass trembles me awake
I lie panting on the shore

There is no line
where the lake ends
and the sky begins.

At nightfall
the lake knows nothing
of our troubles.

She's unconcerned
if I am me or you
or the Queen of England.

To the lake, all is water.
To the sky, all is air.

They intersect
in rainstorms and tussle
over shades of blue.

Unsalted Blue Sunrise

Scalloped clouds
    each pinned
      neatly
    to the Georgia
        O'Keefe sky.

A twentieth-century
    scene
      we walk inside
    looking
      for the lake.

A narrow cloud hangs
center-lake today
like Charlie Brown's bad luck.

But the heron perched
below isn't sad,
being a bird and all.

His neck,
    a question mark,
follows me home.

The Lake Flips the Script

The moon awoke
from its midnight dream
but even without the halo of light
on your little brown dog
I know it's you
with the raveled
imagination. You who search
for violet stones
tucked into my shores.
I write with invisible ink
on the walls of the sky
but you always slice
cucumbers in circles.

Light floods
    a shimmering path
    in water
    beneath the sun.

Perhaps
    a distant
    portal secretly
    submerged.

Oh, to bathe
    in this brilliance
    with fish,
    baptismal!

Yesterday's path
of light today
duplicates
gray skies.

Lake sparkles
leftover sunshine
sequined party skirt
tumbling jagged glass.

The Lake Imagines She's Sky

She never sleeps.
After dark her thoughts are placid,
especially on clear nights.
Staring at a million glinting tea lights
she imagines stars
dressing deep blue waters
in a jewel-studded gown.
She ponders an upside-down life
no mass, no volume
wildlife only travelers
and liquid just passing through.
Nights fill with elegant dreams
but the lake, she's satisfied.

sky paints matching
soft pink rouge
on silent waves
at sunset

powder blue
and blush blend
sky and lake
into one

Sources

Epigraph I: *The Getty Museum.* "Wheatstacks, Snow Effect, Morning" by Claude Monet, https://www.getty.edu/art/collection/object/103RK8 Accessed 10 April 2023.

Epigraph II: Joan Mitchell: *Portrait of an Abstract Painter.* Directed by Marion Cajori, A Christian Blackwood Co-Production, Arthouse Films, 1993, https://www.joanmitchellfoundation.org/joan-mitchell Accessed 10 April 2023.

Epigraph III: Sandburg, Carl. *Abraham Lincoln: The Prairie Years* II, Harcourt, Brace and Company, 1926.

Gratitude to . . .

Joan Franklin Smutny, for giving me poetry.

Rita Griffiths, for the catalyst of inspiration.

Susan Wooldridge, for reminding me to play
with words, for your love of light.

Joshua Corey, for handshakes with the poets
and unwilted insights.

CJ, for writing poems with me again—
in the library.

David Eyman, for ideation and tortoises.

Russell, Lily, and Leona, for making art.

Jennifer Meyer, for your eagle eye.

Julie Isaacson, for a warm welcome.

Kathryn P. Haydon writes poetry to think with fresh eyes and to help turtles run fast. Her poems have been published in *New Croton Review*, *Written River*, *The Bedford Record-Review*, and *Clinch* as well as in books, academic journals, and in her first poetry collection, *What Do Birds Say to the Moon?*

Primarily a non-fiction writer, Kathryn's most recent book is *The Non-Obvious Guide to Being More Creative, No Matter Where You Work*. She writes the column "Adventures in Divergent Thinking" for *Psychology Today* and is the founder of Sparkitivity and Ignite Creative Learning Studio. All of her work is designed to help individuals and teams discover untapped strengths and optimize their most powerful thinking.

Say hello to Kathryn at www.sparkitivity.com.

The Non-Obvious Guide to Being More Creative,
No Matter Where You Work

What Do Birds Say to the Moon?

Creativity for Everybody *with Jane Harvey*

Creatividad para todos *with Jane Harvey*

Discovering and Developing Talents in Spanish-
Speaking Students *with Joan F. Smutny,
Olivia Bolaños, and Gina Danley*

www.ingramcontent.com/pod-product-compliance
Lightning Source LLC
Chambersburg PA
CBHW020605030426
42337CB00013B/1221